Poems of Praise
Volume II

by: John A. McKee

Packaged by Selah Publishing Group, Bristol, TN. The views expressed or implied in this work do not necessarily reflect those of Selah Publishing. Ultimate design, content, and editorial accuracy of this work are the responsibilities of the author.

ISBN 978-1-58930-197-9
Library of Congress Catalog Card Number: 2007904755

Foreword

I have enjoyed writing the poems herein for a little more than thirty years. Written out of a deep, abiding love for my GOD as I was led to write them, my sincerest hope and prayer is that you will find enjoyment in the reading of them.

I dedicate this book of poems to all my Christian brothers and sisters in Christ…May the Light of GOD shine upon you now and forever.

Poems of Praise

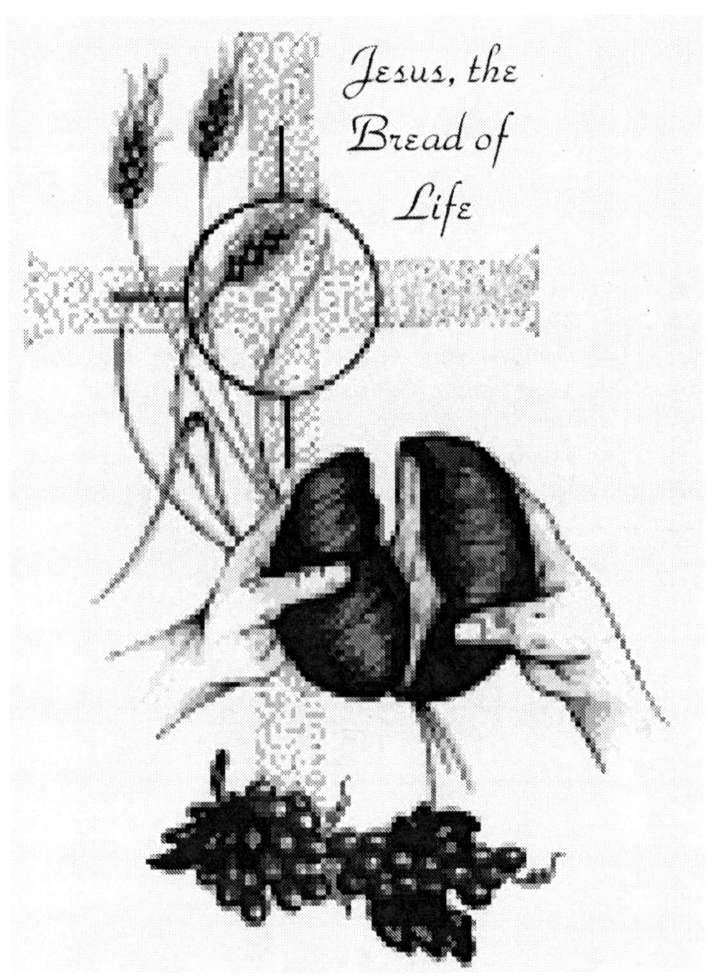

Volume II

Poems of Praise...Volume II

Written out of a deep sense of love and awe to give all Glory and Honor to the Father the Son and the Holy Spirit...

Table of Contents:

ENTRY OF JESUS INTO JERUSALEM

And the multitudes that went before, and that followed, cried, saying, Hosanna to the Son of David: Blessed is he that cometh in the name of the Lord ...Matthew 21:9

Jerusalem, the Holy City

There is a city on a hilltop
Built centuries ago…
A city they named…Jerusalem.

Also called, *'the Holy City'*
By the Chosen Ones of GOD…
Who built a Temple there to worship Him.

And Jesus loved this old city
That was protected by walls…
To keep the enemies of Israel at bay.

When Jesus entered the city
To celebrate the Passover
Palm fronds were strewn along His way.

It was a happy celebration
As the Messiah rode into town
Triumphant upon a colt, foal of an ass.

Zechariah foretold of the scene
In scriptures long before
And his prophecy that day came to pass. *

The Pharisees grew quite jealous
At the adulation given
To Jesus by the throng's joyous praise…

As they sang and danced gaily
Amid the music and laughter
In this celebration lasting for days.

Christ spoke harshly of Pharisees
As He preached to the crowd…
He made no attempt to be discreet.

In righteous indignation
He drove the moneychangers
From the Temple out into the street.

Quoting Isaiah the prophet, **
He lashed them with a whip
For desecrating GOD's House of Prayer.

Chief priests and scribes hearing of this
Then schemed to destroy Him
So angered were they at His teachings there.

*** Zechariah 9:9**
**** Isaiah 56:7 & Psalm 69:9**

by: John A. McKee
February 15, 2005

So we do not Lose Heart

In Paul's second letter
To the Church at Corinth
He offers hope to believers near death.

Giving encouragement to Christians
Remaining faithful to Jesus
Even as they take in their last breath.

He said of our mortal bodies,
"So we do not lose heart."
"Though our outer nature is wasting away..."

He spoke then of our spirits saying…
"Our inner nature,
"Is being renewed every day."

This brief affliction prepares us
For an eternal weight of glory
Beyond anything to be compared…

*"Because we look not to things
"That are seen,"* Paul continued…
"But to things that are unseen…" he declared

*"For the things that are seen
"Are transient,"* wrote Paul,
"But the things that are unseen are eternal." *

We can see our earthly bodies
That houses our unseen spirits…
Because our earthly tents are external.

*"We know while we're home in the body,
"We're away from the Lord,
"For we walk by faith, and not by sight…"*

*"So whether we are at home or away
"We make it our aim to please Him."*
And strive always to do what is right.

For we all shall appear
Before Christ's Judgment Seat
To be judged by GOD's only Son…

He'll separate goats from the sheep
And dispense Holy Justice
In accordance to what we have done. **

The good news for Christians
Is that we have a Counselor
In Christ Jesus…the Judge on His Throne…

He has promised Salvation
To all believers who love Him…
But not to scoffers who refused to atone.

*** II Corinthians 4:16-18**
**** II Corinthians 5:1-10**

by: John A. McKee
February 18, 2005

Jesus blessing the little children
Illustration by Gustave Dore' - (1832-1883)

JESUS BLESSING THE LITTLE CHILDREN

Suffer the little children to come unto me, and forbid them not: for of such is the kingdom of God... (Mark 10: 14)

Come...as a Child

As the sweet little children
Were brought to the Christ
His Disciples tried to keep them at bay.

When the mothers asked Him
To touch their young children
The Lord Jesus did not turn them away.

"Suffer little children
"To come unto me
"And forbid them not..." Jesus said

"For of such is the Kingdom of GOD..." *
Christ continued,
As He gently touched each little head.

The wide-eyed innocence of youth
That's so very compelling
Is lost within just a few years...

Young hearts which were tender
With age can grow callous
Through the hard times, the sadness and tears.

We're warned by Jesus, however,
To not allow that to happen...
We're to come to Him with trust...as a child.

For we have no hope of entering
The Kingdom of GOD
If our hearts have grown hard and defiled.

*** Luke 18:15-17**

by: John A. McKee
March 2, 2005

Just this side of Heaven is a place called *Rainbow Bridge.*
When an animal dies that has been especially close to someone here, that pet goes to Rainbow Bridge.

There are meadows and hills for all of our special friends so they can run and play together. There is plenty of food, water and sunshine, and our friends are warm and comfortable.

All the animals who had been ill and old are restored to health and vigor; those who were hurt or maimed are made whole and strong again, just as we remember them in our dreams of days and times gone by.

The animals are happy and content, except for one small thing; they each miss someone very special to them, who had to be left behind.

They all run and play together, but the day comes when one suddenly stops and looks into the distance. His bright eyes are intent; His eager body quivers. Suddenly he begins to run from the group, flying over the green grass, his legs carrying him faster and faster.

You have been spotted, and when you and your special friend finally meet, you cling together in joyous reunion, never to be parted again. The happy kisses rain upon your face; your hands again caress the beloved head, and you look once more into the trusting eyes of your pet, so long gone from your life but never absent from your heart.

Then you cross *Rainbow Bridge* together....

Author unknown...

Rainbow Bridge

Just on this side of Heaven
There's a place our pets go
To romp and play after they die.

It's called, *'Rainbow Bridge'* …
Filled with trees, shrubs and flowers…
In a garden landscaped in the sky.

The frisky pets there are happy
As they play with each other
Without ever a fight breaking out…

For they're having such fun
Playing ball…chasing Frisbees
That GOD's Angels are tossing about.

They eagerly wait for us there
Within GOD's lovely garden
Free to run without wearing a tether.

They've been told we'll come for them
When our time here is through
And we'll cross *Rainbow Bridge* together

We'll run right into Heaven
Where our loved ones are waiting…
Friends and family who crossed over before.

There Lord Jesus will greet us…
He'll welcome us to GOD's Kingdom
To live blissfully with Him evermore.

by: John A. McKee
March 14, 2005

13

The Apostle, Simon Peter

Simon and his brother Andrew, ,
Made their living by fishing
Upon the blue Sea of Galilee.

As they were casting their net
One day near the shore…
Jesus shouted to them both… *"Follow me…"*

Without hesitating they followed
When the Lord Jesus said,
"And I will make you fishers of men." *
They were the first two Disciples
That He was to call
To help His earthly ministry begin.

Simon was renamed by Jesus
'Cephas'…or, 'Peter'…
The name when translated means… *'rock'…*

Christ said, *"...and upon this 'rock'*
"I will build my Church..." **
Comprised of the Good Shepherd's flock.

Peter was the first of the twelve
To confess with his mouth
That Lord Jesus was GOD's Only Son.

He was also with Him
When Christ was transfigured…
Glowing as bright as the new morning sun.

That day when Jesus walked out
Upon the sea to Disciples
As a storm tossed their boat to and fro…

Only Peter stepped out
To walk to the Master
As the strong winds continued to blow.

Christ said His sheep would be scattered
When they struck down the Shepherd
For Jesus knew that He soon was to die.

Peter responded to Him
He would *never* leave Him…
No…the Lord Jesus he'd *never* deny.

When they arrested the Shepherd
Peter alone drew his sword
To defend Jesus from this disaster.

Although Peter was impetuous
And had his share of flaws
There's no doubting his love for the Master.

*** Matthew 4:18-20**
**** Matthew 16:18**

by: John A. McKee
March 22, 2005

Four Seasons of Life

Springtime, summer and fall
Quickly fade into winter
Which interminably keeps dragging on…

It takes forever, it seems,
For the snow drifts to melt,
And the cold days and nights to be gone.

Have you ever had the thought
Our lives are much like the seasons?
From birth 'til about twenty it's spring…

During our formative years
From babyhood to our teens
We marvel at most *everything.*

Yes, the springtime is grand
For we have brand-new parts …
That feel good and work well as we grow.

And it's amazing how smart
We've become by age twenty …
For there is *nothing* worthwhile we don't know!

But in the heat of the summer
As the years start to build…
Angst and doubt slowly start to creep in.

By now our smugness has left us
For we understand less…
We have troubles right up to our chin.

Through GOD's Grace we work through them
And as the years quickly pass
Quite suddenly, we come into fall…

Our aches and pains have now started
But of life's four distinct seasons…
To my mind, this is the best time of all.

With the kids grown and gone…
There's more time for each other…
And very soon now, we plan to retire.

We'll buy a place in the mountains
Near a lake or a stream…
Enjoy the good life before we expire.

For cold winter soon comes…
As it does to us all…
That time when we feel all alone.

The scriptures take on more meaning
As we come closer to GOD…
For we're nearing the time we'll go home.

by: John A. McKee
March 22, 2005

"I can't wait for Morning…"

The boy was so full life…
Loved by all who knew him
And he responded to them in kind.

He made good grades in school…
Played in the school band…
The lad always was so keen of mind.

But on his way home one day,
He was unsteady of foot…
Little Billy was not feeling good…

His parents became worried…
For He was running a fever
And not acting the way that he should.

It was not the flu or a cold
The boy had contracted
That was making him feel so bad.

The doctor explained to his parents
It was Spinal Meningitis
That their darling son, Billy, had.

As the days turned into weeks
And the weeks into months
Young Billy's condition grew worse…

The lad's demeanor was bright
Though growing weaker each day
Still, he eagerly sought to converse…

When his dad came to his room
To speak with his son
At just before noon one day…

The boy made the remark
About how dark it was getting
In dreamy kind of a way…

"Yes, son, it is getting dark…"
The boy's father replied
As he gently stroked the lad's head.

"I'm getting kind of tired…"
Billy drowsily said…
"Dad, is it time for me to go to bed?"

"Yes, son…you go on to sleep…"
The father said to his son
Choking back his sobs of mourning.

As his life slowly ebbed out,
The boy said to his father…
"Good night, dad…I'll see you in the morning."

I Can't Wait For Morning!

by: John A. McKee
March 22, 2005

19

"Here am I, Lord..." *

"My people are scattered
"Like lost sheep they've wandered
"Their sad cries for help I have heard."

"I seek someone to find them...
"To show them the Way...
"I need someone to bring them the Word."

"Here am I, Lord, send me...
"Let me help find your sheep...
"The lost sinners in need of your aid."

"As you sent someone to me,
"When I was lost in the darkness...
"By myself, all alone and afraid."

"My people hunger and thirst
"For good food and clean water
"I am looking for someone to send."

"Here am I, Lord, send me…
"I'll help them in their need…
"Upon me you know you may depend."

"My people cry out in pain
"For lack of medical care…
"They need someone to go help them out."

"I require doctors and nurses
"And medical technicians…
"I'll provide them with the needed clout ."

"Who will come to assist Me
"Save my suffering people?
"I need volunteers with medical skills…"

"I could do it alone…
"But, I would rather you help me…
"And together, we'll put an end to their ills!"

"Here am I, Lord, send me…
"Let me minister to them
"I will help out wherever I can…"

"I heard your sweet, gentle voice
"Softly calling to me…
"Telling me that I'm a part of your plan."

"I know we haven't much time
"For our lives here are short
"And with more filled sadness than glee…"

"Nonetheless, Sweet Lord Jesus,
"I'm at your beck and call
"Here am I, Lord, won't you send me?"

*** Isaiah 6:8**

by: John A. McKee
April 4, 2005

…Cast the First Stone

How quickly we judge
The misdeeds of others…
How quickly we cast the first stone.

"Do not try to get the speck
"From your brother's eye" Jesus warned,
"Before removing the log from your own." *

We're to search within first …
Self-examine our hearts…
Confessing before GOD in prayer.

Asking Him to forgive
Our many weighty transgressions
Which are too heavy for us to bear.

Because none are immune,
We have all fallen short…
And we each stand convicted of sin.

But if we seek absolution…
If we repent of our wrongdoing,
We are one with our GOD once again.

It is so wonderfully peaceful,
This simple act of atonement…
To be forgiven through GOD's Holy Grace.

Not some time in the future
But right here and now…
While in prayer… right here in this place.

Christ commands we forgive
All who trespass against us…
Which is where we must always start.

For we shall not be forgiven
Our many sins against GOD
When we harbor ill will in our heart.

As He forgave the adulteress
Dragged into His presence
By some self-righteous men long ago…

So the Lord shall forgive us
When we earnestly seek Him
For the Lord Jesus Christ told us so.

*** Matthew 7:1-5**
**** Matthew 6:14, 15**

by: John A. McKee
April 6, 2005

23

"Lo, I tell you a Mystery…"

After lying three days
In a borrowed tomb,
The Lord Jesus emerged resurrected…

His victory over death
Was a triumph for Christians
But to the Pharisees…subterfuge was suspected.

So they bribed Roman guards
To say His body was stolen
By His Disciples in the darkness of night.

In truth, the terrified guards
At seeing the risen Lord Jesus,
Had fainted as dead men in fright. *

For the resurrection of Jesus
Was a miraculous event…
The linchpin of GOD's holy plan

To give joyful encouragement
To Disciples and followers
Of Christ Jesus…the Son of Man.

GOD has a gift for each Christian
On the day of joyous Rapture
When the Messiah returns with a shout!

The gift of imperishable bodies
That neither grow old nor faint
Paul wrote the Corinthians about… **

"Lo, I tell you a mystery…"
"…We shall all be changed…"
"In the twinkling of an eye…"

When the last trumpet sounds,
The Church Bride of Lord Jesus
Shall be gathered to Him in the sky.

"Death is swallowed up by victory."
Paul quotes in his letter…
For His resurrection changed everything.

"O death, where is thy victory?"
Paul continued the quote,
"O death…where is thy sting?"

*** Matthew 28:1-15**
**** I Corinthians 15:50-55**

by: John A. McKee
April 17, 2005

"You have heard that it was said…" *

"You have heard that it was said
"To the men of old . . .
"That you shall not kill…" Christ declared.

"But I say to you,
"Anyone angry with his brother
"From GOD's Judgment may not be spared." **

"You have heard that it was said
"That you shall not commit adultery…"
Then He gave His listeners a start…

"But I say to you that anyone
"Who looks lustfully at a woman
"Has committed adultery with her in his heart." **

Six times Jesus told them,
"You have heard that it was said…"
And each time after speaking that phrase…

26

He would quote a law to them
Which they all knew by rote,
And each time the bar He would raise…

Saying, *"But I say to you"*
As He raised the bar
To expand upon what was expected.

Christ was convicting mankind
Of our sinful nature,
For by sin every heart is infected.

We have all fallen short
Of what our GOD expects…
He wants us all to strive to be better.

We're to make a strong effort
To obey the law's spirit…
And not just live up to it's letter.

Then He'll help us understand
That the purpose and nature
Of the Law in GOD's Divine Plan…

Is to teach and instruct us
On what we must do
To live in harmony with our fellow man.

GOD's instructions, when followed,
Will enrich our lives…
If we ignore them our lives shall diminish.

His Law helps to maintain
A calm heart that's at peace
From the start of the race to the finish.

*** Matthew 5:21-42**
**** (Paraphrase)**

by: John A. McKee
April 30, 2005

Triumph of the Spirit

The Holy Spirit indwells
The hearts of GOD's people
To protect us from all that defiles.

And through the darkest of hours
The Spirit within
Can brighten grim faces with smiles.

It is a mystery to man
How this can be so...
Quite often we're awed by this fact...

As we see tragedy unfold
That's heart breaking to witness
And see the different ways people react.

When disaster befalls some,
They rise bravely above it
To conquer the challenge they face.

They give us inspiration
By setting an example
That's reflective of GOD's Holy Grace.

The Muslim terrorist attack
On September 11th...
Crashing planes into New York's Twin Towers...

Was a crime perpetrated
By evil, misguided men...
Willing pawns of satanic powers.

Shocked and angered Americans,
Incensed at the carnage...
As a people became unified...

Strangers from all walks of life
Began search and rescue,
Through the rubble and debris side by side...

The triumph of the Spirit
Was manifest by the actions
Of heroic rescuers and victims alike.

Some sacrificed their lives
In their quest for survivors
Of that horrific, cruel and cowardly strike.

The attack didn't destroy
The spirit of America
As the murderers had hoped that it would,

Indeed it brought us together
And turned many to GOD
As only tragedy of this magnitude could.

by: John A. McKee
May 10, 2005

*And I looked, and behold a pale horse: and his
name that sat on him was death. Revelation 6:8*

Behold, a Pale Horse...

He was caught up in the spirit
To be shown many things
To happen just as GOD has planned.

He described Heavenly things
Seen in GOD's Revelation
Which are hard for us to understand…

For many things he was shown
Were of a symbolic nature
And thus, subject to interpretation.

We read what Saint John has written
In the last book of the Bible
The book most people call *Revelation*.

Blessed is he who reads
John's words of prophecy
And blessed are those who hear,

And blessed are those who keep
What is written therein,
John said, *'For the time is near.'* *

He transcribed seven letters
Dictated by Jesus
To the Churches in existence that day.

Christ gave mixed praises to some,
While admonishing others
Whom He faulted for falling away.

For they had not kept the faith…
Had eaten of offerings to idols…
Some held to the teachings of Balaam.

After this, John was called
Before GOD's mighty throne
To be shown of things yet to come…

He described GOD on His throne,
Likened to earthly treasures
To impart to us the beauty he saw…

But mere words cannot capture
The magnificence of GOD
That held John, the Apostle, in awe.

The Lamb would open the scroll
Containing seven seals
Enabling John to view future events.

And he described scenes that he saw
After each seal was opened
That were graphically, very intense.

When the first seal was opened,
He saw a conqueror riding
On a white horse with a bow and a crown.

As the second seal was opened
A rider upon a red horse
Caused men to strike each other down.

A rider appeared with a balance
Riding on a black horse
After the Lamb opened up the third seal …

And when the fourth seal was opened…
Behold, a pale horse…
Whose grim rider held no appeal…

For the fourth horseman was *'Death'*
And Hades followed him…
Over 1/4 of the earth they had power

To kill with not just the sword,
But through famine and pestilence…
And allowing the wild beasts to devour.

*** Rev 1:10 – 5:8 (Paraphrased)***

by: John A. McKee
May 12, 2005

31

Speak to me, O Lord *

As I listened for GOD
In the midst of the storm
He was nowhere to be found in the wind…

Yet, from within my heart
My GOD comforted me…
He's my Rock upon whom I depend.

After the wind had abated
An earthquake began
But the Lord GOD was not in the quake…

As it broke rock into pieces…
And split gaping fissures
It caused everything near it to shake.

Following the earthquake
A fire consumed and destroyed...
But my GOD was not in the fire.

After the fire in the silence,
Came His still, small voice
To instruct...to give hope... to inspire.

Speak to me, O Lord,
This wretched, unworthy sinner
That Satan tries so hard to snare.

Calm my troubled heart...
Grant me your perfect peace
That soothes away my every care.

Speak to me, O Lord,
I long for your instruction
Each minute of each hour of each day.

I seek your unerring guidance
For *you* are the Potter...
And I, Lord...I'm only the clay.

Speak to me, O Lord,
Let me hear your still voice
Over the thundering roar of life's storm...

Guide me by your Light
Through this evil old world...
Keep my loved ones and me from all harm.

Speak to me, O Lord
You're my GOD and my King...
Before the world I will never deny it...

Here am I, Lord, your servant...
Listening in the silence...
For your small voice so soft and so quiet.

*** I Kings 19:11-13**

by: John A. McKee
July 15, 2005

How can we be Sure?

Have you ever had doubts
About where you will go
When your life on this earth is through?

Have you ever had thoughts
That the life everlasting
Is for others…but not meant for you?

How can we be sure
That we are to be saved…
Knowing how wayward we've been?

We've all lived our lives
As though it did not matter
How much we have wallowed in sin.

Calling it *'indiscretions of youth'*…
Or, simply, doing *'our thing'*…
Maybe we were just *'having a blast'*.

To receive life everlasting
Here is what you *must* do…
Seek forgivness for your sinful past.

You've heard of *'Repentance'*
Since you were a youth
Without thinking just what it entailed…

It means you resolve before GOD
To turn your life around
In the areas where you have failed.

For all have fallen short
Of the Glory of GOD…*
Because each of us gives in to sin.

But that does not mean
Life Eternal in Heaven
Is a prize that we'll never win…

So, *how can we be sure*
That we're to be saved?
And just what does *redemption* mean?

It is the path to *salvation*
And Jesus spells it out for us
In the Gospel of John 3:16…

"For GOD so loved the world
"That He gave His only Son…"
"That whoever believes in Him"

"Should not perish" He said,
"But have eternal life…" ******
That's His **PROMISE**…it's not just a whim.

*** Romans 3:23**
**** John 3:16**

by: John A. McKee
July 16, 2005

To GOD be the Glory

The Glory of GOD
Is manifest in Jesus,
Since He and the Father are one.

And GOD's plan for redemption
Is for all who confess
Christ Jesus is His only Son...

His plan was fulfilled
On a cross at *'Golgotha'*...
As His Crucified Son died in disgrace.

GOD's Lamb without blemish
Surrendered His life
For the sins of the whole human race.

For Him to love us *that much,*
Though our transgressions be scarlet...
Is so hard for my mind to conceive...

But, our faith in GOD's Word
In the Old and New Testaments
Gives us Good News that we can believe.

Yes, the Glory of GOD
Is passed on to the Son
He showed it in a number of ways...

For after the Lord Jesus died
And was placed in a tomb...
Resurrected, He arose in three days.

He had promised His Disciples
That this would take place
But, Even so, it gave them quite a start...

When He appeared suddenly to them,
Though His countenance had changed...
Each knew this was Christ in his heart.

He remained forty days with them
To encourage and instruct...
They were joyful...no longer in grief.

While they were gathered about Him
He ascended to Heaven
As they stared transfixed in disbelief.

by: John A. McKee
July 30, 2005

The Great Fall *

"How you are fallen from Heaven
"O Day Star…son of Dawn!
"How you are cast down to the ground,"

"I will be like the Most High."
Satan said in his heart…
Greater arrogance shall never be found.

"I will ascend into Heaven,"
"Above the stars of GOD
"I will set my throne on high."

Satan was a powerful Archangel
Given charge over many
Who made a conscious decision to defy

The Sovereignty of GOD
By seeking equality with Him
The great mystery to me, is…***why?***

"I will ascend above
"The heights of the clouds.
"I will make myself like the Most High."

When the Archangel, Michael
Did battle with him
Michael prevailed over him in the fight. **

For inciting rebellion in Heaven
GOD cast Satan to earth…
Forever banished from His Holy sight.

When Satan chose to rebel
By usurping GOD's rule…
That was an unpardonable sin.

Friends, if Satan could beguile Angels…
For one third of them followed…
It's small wonder all *mankind* gives in.

His sin stemmed from the arrogance
Of inflated self-esteem…
Satan became overly filled with pride.

We would do well to examine
Our own hearts to see
If *we* have that sin lurking inside.

*** Isaiah 14:12-15**
**** Rev 12:7-12**
by: John A. McKee
August 1, 2005

The Aaronic Benediction *

Aaron was appointed by GOD
As the first high priest...
To prepare and present all offerings. **

He was forerunner of Jesus
In his role as high priest
And a 'Shadow of Heavenly things' ***

His sons were to follow
Within the priesthood…
And Moses anointed them, too.

They assisted their father
In the Tent of Meeting
As only ordained priests could do…

Offering sacrificed animals
To GOD for His people
To atone for commission of sin.

But then they would backslide
And sacrifice more animals
To seek GOD's forgiveness again.

GOD gave directions to Moses
To instruct Aaron, his brother,
To bless His people in a particular way…

A blessing still used by pastors
Following the sermons
In many Churches worldwide today.

The benediction begins…
'The Lord bless and keep you'…
Through GOD's Holy Grace we are blessed.

'The Lord make His face to shine upon you
'And be gracious to you…'
Gentle words to put our minds at rest.

'The Lord lift up His Countenance
The benediction concludes…
'Upon you, and give you peace'.

The last phrase is meant
To comfort GOD's people
Giving their troubled hearts sweet release.

*** Leviticus 8, 9**
**** Numbers 6:22-27**
***** Hebrews 8**

by: John A. McKee
August 6, 2005

Desert Showers

The thunder rumbled and rolled
As the lightening flashed
Illuminating darkened skies…

After so long without rain
It was a welcome sight
To every desert dweller's eyes.

For the rain cooled the air
Giving temporary relief
From the blazing hot summer sun.

In a mad dash to their cars,
Many shoppers got drenched
But all seemed to be having great fun.

Squealing with delight
They splashed through rain puddles
Searching pockets or purses for keys

And saying a prayer in their hearts
To thank GOD for the rain,
That enabled the long drought to ease.

He's an awesome GOD
Who fulfills the needs
Of all life within His creation…

And He seeks our assistance
To help the less fortunate
Facing hard times…perhaps desolation.

Just as He causes the rain
To fall from the Heavens…
So GOD moves us to do His will.

When we aid those in need
It soon becomes habit…
A habit GOD asks us to instill

For as refreshing rain showers
Upon the parched desert
Give relief to life indwelling there…

So compassionate aid
Dispensed freely with love
Brings relief to those in need of our care.

by: John A. McKee
August 9, 2005

"To him who Conquers…"

In the Revelation to John
Jesus spoke words of promise
To John's present, his future and past.

Dictating letters to John
To the first seven Churches…
Christ commanded each one to hold fast.

He adjures in His letters
That they are to *'conquer'*...
To be faithful to Him to the end. *

We're to follow His precepts...
Walk on His lighted path...
For only His righteous path will ascend.

"Be faithful unto death...
"And I'll give you 'The crown of life '."
The early Church in Ephesus was told.

"I shall make him a pillar
"In the Temple of my GOD..."
Said the Christ to His Philadelphia fold.

"To eat of the Tree of Life
"In the Paradise of GOD."
Where tears never more fill our eyes...

Written in all seven letters
Was the phrase, *"He who conquers..."*
Those who withstand the *'Father of Lies'*.

"I will not blot his name
"From the Book of Life... "
"He who conquers shall be clad thus in white...."

"I will grant him to sit
"With me on my throne..."
Said GOD's Son...the One called *The Light*.

He warns us to repent...
To be ever faithful...
For one day He'll arrive as a thief.

We know not the day or the hour
Christ will return here in *Triumph!*
So...*Conquer*...hold fast your belief.

*** Revelation 2, 3**

by: John A. McKee
August 13, 2005

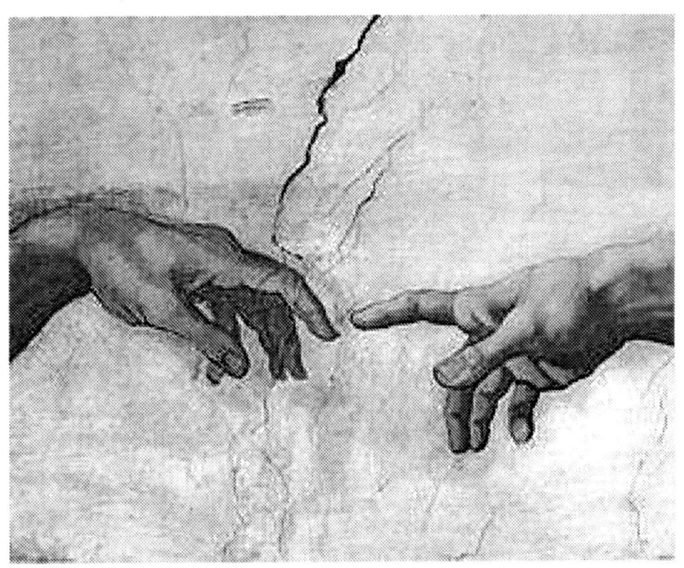

Life is but a Vapor...

During Job's terrible suffering
He said, *"...My life is a breath..."* *
In his anguish he tried to explain...

By lamenting his life
"...As a cloud fades and vanishes..."
He prayed earnestly to GOD in his pain.

Although mortal life *is* brief
It leads to life everlasting
For all who accept Christ as King...

Who acknowledge Him as Lord
As Son of GOD and as Savior...
Who arose victorious over mortal death's sting.

Man's life is but a vapor...
A mere wisp of smoke...
Quickly over as though it were a dream.

It is just one grain of sand
On the beach of eternity...
No matter *how* important we make it seem.

We make big plans for tomorrow...
Self-assured we'll be there...
When, in fact, that may not be in GOD's plan.

James warns us in his letter
Such self-centered behavior
Is regarded as *arrogance* in man. **

It *is good* to make plans...
But we're to seek GOD's will...*first*
And if it *is* His will...let it be so.

Far too often we ignore
What *He*'d have us to do
In a vain effort to build up our ego.

Such boastfulness is evil...
This disdain for GOD's will...
When we know it's the right thing do.

Repent of this sinful action...
Seek the Lord GOD's forgiveness...
And He'll reveal what His plans are for you.

*** Job 7:7-9**
**** James 4: 13-17**

by: John A. McKee
August 15, 2005

Boy Jesus in the Temple

When Jesus was a lad
Of but twelve years of age,
He journeyed to Jerusalem. *

It was His family's tradition
To attend the feast of the Passover
And each year He attended with them.

When the feast had concluded,
They began the trek home…
Unaware Jesus had lingered behind.

48

After the first day of travel,
They realized He was missing,
But the Boy, Jesus…no one could find.

Three days later, they found Him…
In the Temple with teachers
Listening to, and asking questions of them.

All who heard Him were *amazed*
At the Boy's understanding…
And *Astonished* by answers from Him.

"Son, why have you treated us so?"
A distraught Mary said,
"Your father and I have been looking for you."

"Did you not know," Jesus said
"That I must be in my Father's House?"
Hinting at what He had come here to do.

Both Mary and Joseph knew
What Jesus had meant…
The others thought He was just having fun.

Mary kept these things in her heart
Recalling Gabriel had told her
She would give birth to GOD's Only Son.

As Jesus grew in stature
He also increased in wisdom…
Finding favor with both GOD and man.

He was obedient unto death…
Crucified for our sins…
In accordance to GOD's Holy Plan.

*** Luke 2:41-52**

by: John A. McKee
August 16, 2005

49

Saint John, the Baptist

We know little about John…
Also known as, *'the Baptist'*…
Of whom Isaiah, the Prophet, foretold.

We know he prepared the way
For the Lord Jesus Christ.
And John the Baptist was incredibly *bold*.

Living in the harsh wilderness,
He ate locusts and wild honey
And wore a robe made of animal skin.

Roaming throughout Judea
With his following of Disciples
It's unclear with just how many men.

He preached to workers and soldiers
Religious leaders and others
And encouraged them all to repent.

John was waist-deep in the Jordon
Baptizing both Jews *and* Gentiles…
When the Lord Jesus Christ to him went.

As Jesus waded up to him
And asked to be baptized,
John said Jesus should be baptizing *him*.

John knew GOD had sent Christ
For mankind's salvation
He was blameless…this Lamb without sin.

But the Pharisees and Sadducees
He called a *"brood of vipers"*…
Who must repent, for they were sinful men.

John chastised Herod Antipas…
Galilee's governor…
Causing that arrogant man much chagrin.

For John boldly told Herod
He was breaking GOD's law
Taking Herodias…his brother Philip's wife.

The Governor placed John in prison
At Herodias' insistence.
She demanded Herod take Saint John's life.

When Herodias' daughter, Salome,
Danced at his birthday banquet…
After she'd danced, Herod drunkenly said,

'You may have anything you ask for…
'Up to half of my kingdom.'
Herodias told her to ask for John's head.

by: John A. McKee
August 16, 2005

'*In GOD we Trust*'

When our forefathers authored
The US Constitution,
Their concept was radically new.

For the government they formed
Of, by and for the people…
Embodied the Judeo-Christian view.

The motto, *'In GOD We Trust'*
Stamped on U.S. currency
Congress enacted in eighteen sixty four...

Historically, most politicians
Were GOD-fearing Christians…
But that's rarely the case anymore.

Many Supreme Court rulings
Over the past several decades
Fill most Christians with deep disgust.

For they have ruled evil…as good,
And pronounced good…to be evil
Declaring their liberal decisions are *just.*

I speak of legalized abortion…
The prayer ban in our schools
Forbidding teaching of GOD's Creation.

If they allow atheistic teaching
Of Darwin's *theory* as *fact*…
Perhaps a monkey *is* their relation!

The Prophet, Isaiah, has warned
Of GOD's wrath to come…
Upon all who twist things around. *

That smug, arrogant faction
Someday shall pay for their actions…
Before GOD when *true* justice is found.

For GOD *will not* be mocked.
There's a price to be paid…
And America will yet rue the day

The liberal courts were allowed
To overturn core Christian values
Giving agnostics and atheists their way.

*** Isaiah 5:20-23**

by: John A. McKee
August 30, 2005

Prayer and Confession *

In the letter of James,
He concluded his letter
Extolling the power of prayer.

For he had witnessed first-hand
The tender mercies of Jesus
As eyewitness to His deep love and care.

On the days when we're cheerful
We should show Him we're grateful
By singing to our GOD in praise.

For it's a benevolent Father
Who provides us good humor
Upon even our less than good days.

We're to summon Church Elders
For one suffering an illness
Which they can no longer endure.

Elders will anoint them with oil
In the name of Lord Jesus,
And offer a prayer to our GOD for their cure.

The sick shall be healed
And forgiven their sins
If they repent of their sins by confessing.

James said confess one to another…
And pray for each other
To be healed through GOD's Holy blessing.

GOD responds to the righteous
As they earnestly pray…
For a prayer from the righteous has power.

Elijah was just such a man…
He prayed fervently to GOD
Asking GOD to withhold the rain shower

And for three years and six months
It *didn't* rain on this earth
As punishment for King Ahab's sin…

Then once more Elijah prayed…
Only *this* time *for* rain…
And the earth brought forth its fruit again.

If one wanders from the truth…
And is brought back to the Light
Even as he takes his last breath…

The person leading that sinner
Will cover a multitude of sins.
Thereby saving his own soul from death

*** James 5:13-20**

by: John A. McKee
September 1, 2005

55

The River of Life

Come to the River…
The *River of Life*…
Drink deeply of the water found there.

The *'Living Water'* from Jesus
Quenches spiritual thirst
Each time we seek Him in prayer.

He who drinks *Living Water*
Given freely by GOD
Shall never be thirsty again…

Christ said this to the woman
That He met at the well,
Whom He knew to be living in sin.

"It shall become within him
As a spring of water
*Welling up to eternal life." **

A life of comfort and peace
In the Kingdom of GOD…
A life devoid of all sorrow and strife.

Jesus said, *"If anyone thirst,*
*"Let him come to me and drink." ****
Giving many of His listeners a start…

"He who believes in me,
"As the scriptures has said,
"…Living waters shall flow from his heart."

He was speaking of the Spirit
On the last day of the feast
Who would fill all of those who believe.

After Jesus was glorified
The Holy Spirit *was* sent
And His Disciples were the first to receive.

So, lift your voices in song
And give praise to the Lord…
For He has saved us from sin…set us *free.*

"I am the Way," said Lord Jesus,
"The Truth and the Life…
*"No one comes to the Father but through me." ******

*** John 4:13**
**** John 7:37-39**
***** John 14:6**

by: John A. McKee
September 22, 2005

THE LAST JUDGMENT

And I saw the dead, small and great, stand before God; and the books were opened: and another book was opened, which is the book of life... (Revelation 20:12)

Final Judgment

"Jesus, remember me
"When you come into your Kingdom."
Said a crucified thief at His side.

"Truly, I say to you,
"Today you'll be with me
"In Paradise." Lord Jesus replied. *

The word...*'Paradise'*...Jesus used
To the penitent thief...
He used as a synonym for Heaven.

Saint Paul spoke of Paradise
In Second Corinthians 12:4... **
As did Saint John in Revelation 2:7.

GOD has reserved Paradise
As a place for believers...
On this, the Bible has much to tell. ***

The righteous have always
Gone to Paradise (or Heaven),
And the wicked to Hades (or Hell).

Both of these places
Are but "temporary residence"
Until that day when Christ is to return

In majestic power and glory
With His angelic host...
That moment for which Christians yearn.

He'll judge the quick and the dead
From the *'Book of Life'* contents...
Each judgment to be based upon deeds.

Those whose names Christ finds written
To the life everlasting...
Those not written will be burned as weeds.

And this is the second death.
Eternal damnation.
To burn forever in the *'Lake of Fire'*. ****

GOD at that time shall create
A new Heaven and earth
And the first Heaven and earth will expire *****

*** Luke 23:42-43**
**** II Corinthians 12:4**
***** Matthew 25:31-46**
****** Rev 20:11-15**
******* Rev 20:11-15**
by: John A. McKee
October 1, 2005

GOD's Choices

GOD chooses the lowly,
The despised, the weak…
And the foolish to heap shame the wise.

GOD's foolishness is wiser
Than the wisdom of man
Which is but folly in our Holy GOD's eyes. *

Moses was slow of speech…
Not an eloquent speaker,
Yet he was chosen by GOD to lead.

He brought *GOD's Chosen People*
From the bondage of Pharaoh,
With GOD's help…Moses was to succeed. **

David was smallest in stature
Of Jesse's eight sons,
But it was he whom GOD was to choose ***

To become king over Israel
After the death of King Saul
And in battle…he was never to lose.

Of the two daughters of Laben,
Rachel was the beauty
But *Leah* was plain with weak eyes. ****

Jacob married them both
And Leah bore him six sons
Her sister, Rachel came to despise.

GOD had blessed Leah with children
For she felt so unloved
And GOD knew that her heart was pure…

Although her sons became leaders
Of five tribes in Israel
Her heartache was hard to endure.

All throughout the scriptures
GOD has chosen to use
The unseemly, the meek and the mild…

Even His Son, the *Lord Jesus*,
He sent to save us from sin
Was sent here as a weak mortal child.

Just consider the *Disciples*
That Christ Jesus chose…
None of the twelve men had a PHD.

They were quite ordinary men,
But were dedicated to *Him*…
Which is just what He wants us to be.

*** I Corinthians 1:18 – 2:16**
**** Exodus 4:10**
***** I Samuel 16:6-13**
****** Genesis 29:9-30:29**

by: John A. McKee
October 5, 2005

Children of GOD

Take time each day
To smell the roses,
And never forget to smile.

Say hello to a stranger…
Do a kind deed for someone
And walk for them one extra mile.

For each day is a gift
From a Benevolent GOD,
That we're given by Him to enjoy.

Whether we're aged grandparents…
Or middle-aged parents…
Perhaps still just a young girl or boy.

You see, to Him we're *all* children,
Whom He loves as His own
Wanting only what's best for each child.

GOD sends His Holy Spirit
To dwell within hearts
Of lost sinners who have become reconciled.

You ask, how do we become
Reconciled with our GOD?
Just repent…for He is quick to forgive.

Accept His Son, Jesus Christ,
As your Lord and Savior
Change the sinful way that you now live.

That's called, 'repentance of sin',
Which can be hard to do,
With Satan whispering…"*sin is all right*".

But, when you make your commitment
To give your life to Lord Jesus
Satan cannot prevail in that fight.

Though he'll try harder each day
To lure you away
From the path you have chosen to trod…

The *'Father of Lies'* cannot win
He won't deceive you again…
Now you're one of the *'Children of GOD'*.

by: John A. McKee
October 14, 2005

End Times

The Bible paints a grim picture
Of end-times on earth
And Christ warns us to watch for the signs.

As we draw closer each day
To the Messiah's return,
Events unfold just as Jesus defines.

Many deceivers shall appear…
Claiming Jesus Christ's name
Leading many of His sheep astray.

We're to remain steadfast
Through the turmoil and troubles
In this evil world day after day…

He said we'd hear of wars
And rumors of wars…
Of pestilence…famine…earthquakes. *

The faint of heart shall falter
And fall away from their faith
But *His* faithful, Christ never forsakes. **

During the time of tribulation
Many shall follow their lusts ***
And evil shall wax ever worse ****

It will be a time of difficulty
For those with child
As panicky people take flight and disburse. *****

Peter said there will be scoffers
Who won't care to hear
Of the Savior's victorious return…

When He comes as a thief
Heaven shall then pass away
And the earth and all in it shall burn. ******

For there will be a *new* Heaven
And a *new earth* as well
After these things have all come to pass. *******

And Christ will rule over all
From His Great White Throne…
Upon a *Crystal Sea of Glass*. ********

*** Matthew 24:5-7 (KJV)**
**** I Tim 4:1-2**
***** Jude:16-18**
****** II Tim 3:13**
******* Matthew 24:16-21**
******** II Peter 3:1-10**
********* Rev 21:1**
********** Rev 4:1-6**

by: John A. McKee
October 18, 2005

Heroes for GOD

There have been *heroes for GOD*
All down through the ages
Urging men to repent of their sin.

Among Old Testament heroes
Was a man they called, Daniel,
Who was cast into a lion's den. *

For he'd refused to worship
King Darius as a god…
He petitioned *his* Lord GOD instead.

The king tossed and turned
Without sleep all that night
Fearing Daniel was probably dead.

But GOD had sent His Angel
To shut the mouths of the lions
And they immediately became serene.

The king was tricked into signing
The edict to be worshipped
By men who were jealous and mean.

They knew Darius favored Daniel
And had plans to promote him
As overseer of *all* things in the realm…

So they plotted their scheme
To rid themselves of Daniel
Not wishing to see him at the helm.

The king hastened to the den
At the first light of dawn
Anxious to see how young Daniel had fared.

When He saw him *alive*
The king cried out for *joy*...
Through GOD's Grace, Daniel's life had been spared.

As He was removed from the den
With no hurt from the lions...
King Darius had his accusers arrested.

And *they* were thrown to the lions
Along with their families...
For this evil deed the king so detested.

With GOD's Angel now gone
The lions were no longer tranquil
And attacked...breaking each victim's bones.

The scene suddenly grew quiet
With the only sounds to be heard
Were low growls from the lions and groans.

King Darius restored Daniel
To his former position...
Who GOD *was*...the king made very clear.

He wrote another decree declaring:
Before Daniel's GOD
Every person must tremble and fear...

For He is the One Living GOD
Who endures forever
Whose Kingdom shall not be destroyed.

The GOD of Daniel had saved him
From the power of the lions
And prosperity Daniel once more enjoyed.

*** Daniel 6**

by: John A. McKee
October 21, 2005

67

Communing with GOD

I climbed a mountain one day
To commune with my GOD
And after reaching the highest peak…

I knelt down on my knees
Beneath the aspens and pines
And listened for the Lord GOD to speak.

As the wind softly blew
Through His beautiful trees
With His birds singing sweetly above…

GOD spoke to my heart
In a calm, soothing manner…
Reassuring me of His infinite love.

I put out to sea in a sloop
To commune with my GOD…
Just me…with His seagulls and fish.

I listened intently for Him
In that serene setting
As whitecaps crested with a gentle…*swish*.

I said a prayer of thanksgiving
For His bountiful blessings
As I steered the small boat with the wheel.

He sent the Holy Spirit to me
Who filled my troubled heart
With a genuine peace I could *feel*.

I went aloft in a balloon
To commune with my GOD
And while I soared all alone in the sky…

I prayed that He would forgive me
My past scarlet sins
As I watched the landscape drifting by.

But we needn't go to these places
To commune with our GOD
For He's been with us right from the start…

We may rest assured…*always*
That He hears every word…
For He resides with us deep in our heart.

by: John A. McKee
October 31, 2005

69

Fly above the Storm

That we are blessed as a people
To have a GOD who loves us
By many, is a truth understood.

For He guides us through trials
We encounter in life
As only a loving GOD could.

Storms of life can strike quickly,
Often without any warning
And immobilize us through stark fear.

But it's a comfort to know
That we're not in it alone…
It's a comfort to know GOD is near.

During those times it's important
That we seek His counsel
That we thankfully praise Him in prayer.

For the surest way possible
To have a heart that's at peace
Is give to Him the burdens we bear.

Let Him remove all those burdens,
For our GOD is *awesome*…
There is *nothing* that He cannot do.

He is the Author of Life.
He is Creator of all.
Irrespective of the atheist's view.

It may be a natural disaster
Or some personal problem
That makes our inner turmoil begin.

Illness could be the issue…
There are any *number* of trials
Perhaps causal of the storms we are in.

Take to wing as a bird
And fly above that storm
That's disrupting your life in some way.

For there is help to be had
From our Lord GOD on high…
He is awaiting you this very day.

by: John A. McKee
November 10, 2005

For Thine is the Power

Father, I ask you to bless
The one reading this…
Please minister to them today.

Displace their pain and suffering…
Their destructive self-doubt
With your Grace and Peace, Lord, I pray.

Provide them the confidence needed
To overcome their fear
Of reaching out to your sheep who are lost.

When they tire to exhaustion
Lord, help them understand
They're to witness for you at all cost.

Grant them the patience and strength
To be humbly submissive…
Bend to *your* will in all that they do.

Where there's spiritual stagnation
Condition their hearts
To be aflame in their love for you.

Where they are fearful and anxious
Lord, bolster their courage…
Enable them to triumph over strife.

Where they're steeped in sin, Lord
Break those sinful bonds
And lead them toward a more righteous life.

O Lord, bless their finances
And grant them clear vision
To see what you'd have them to do.

Raise up leaders and friends
To encourage and support them
When the evil one attempts to subdue.

Give them the discernment
To recognize that evil
And to *resist* it…*for Thine is the Power…*

To defeat *'the Father of Lies'*
Who roars about like a lion
Seeking out those whom he would devour. *

*** I Peter 5:8**

*We ask all these things in the name of Jesus Christ,
our Lord and Savior and for His sake…amen.*

by: John A. McKee
November 14, 2005

73

Thanks be to GOD

God, I bow humbly before you
To give thankful praise
In gratitude for your tender grace

And for the Lord Jesus Christ
Who demonstrated His love
By sacrificing His life in my place.

My grateful thanks also,
For this day you have made…
For allowing me to live my life free.

All thanks and praise to you
For the undeserved love
You bestow every day upon me.

Thank you for the warm sun,
The blue earth and bright moon
Inspiring writers of both poem and song.

Everything in existence
Was wrought by your hand…
The *creation* detractors are *wrong*.

We give thanks for the stars
And myriad Heavenly bodies
Created not by the *'Big Bang'*…but by *you*.

You alone, Lord, are worthy
Of all honor and glory
For out of chaos, you made all things new.

How can *anyone* doubt
Your majesty and power
When they view all the things you have done?

How can *anyone* disbelieve
That through your love for us
You'd selflessly sacrifice your Son?

"For GOD so loved the world,
"That He gave His only Son…" *
Who was to die on a cross for *our* sin.

How can we ever repay
The huge debt that we owe?
A prayer of thanks is the way to begin…

*** John 3:16**

by: John A. McKee
November 18, 2005

Look unto the Hills...

"I will lift up mine eyes
"Unto the hills,
"From whence does my help come?"

"My help comes from the Lord
"Who made Heaven and earth."
The Psalmist wrote in Psalm 121.

As we journey through life
We have GOD as our refuge...
To comfort us each time we call.

Giving His blessed assurance
That He'll be with us always
To support us lest we should fall.

He neither slumbers nor sleeps.
His sure step never falters
On that rocky road we walk each day.

He'll not let our feet slip
On this rough road of life…
As gently, He leads us His way.

Yes, the Lord GOD is our keeper…
Sole protector from evil
That's rampant in all of the nations…

And becoming ever more so
As the earth spins on its axis
In endless twenty-four hour rotations.

Though it may appear GOD is sleeping
That is certainly not so.
He watches over us as only He can.

Let your faith remain *steadfast*…
Do not allow it to waver…
While He works at fulfilling His Plan

Hold tight to that thought
As you journey life's road
For at the end of that road is…*the prize*.

Life eternal in Heaven
With the Trinity and loved ones…
Never more any tears or goodbyes.

by: John A. McKee
November 22, 2005

Imperishable Body

As the years swiftly pass
A transformation occurs
Upon approaching our *'twilight years.'*

Skin becomes wrinkled and thin…
Hair turns gray…or is lost
Youthful vigor we enjoyed disappears.

We're reduced now in stature
Due to shrinkage of disks
That cushions vertebrae in our spine.

This creates such discomfort
Many develop a stoop…
Enduring pain that is hard to define.

And that's just the beginning…
It gets worse every year.
When arthritis attacks vulnerable knees

It becomes painful to climb
Up steep stairs anymore
Without stopping on each step to wheeze.

Hips begin causing you pain…
Eyesight grows ever dimmer
Making it hard to see anything clear.

We turn the volume up high
When watching TV,
For by now…we can just barely hear.

I don't paint this bleak picture
Of gloom and doom as a lark…
Or to bring your spirits down low.

I'm simply making a point
Of our human frailties
To preface good news you should know.

The mortal bodies we indwell
Are but *'tents'* Peter said.
Which one day are to be put aside…*

At the *Rapture,* when Christians
Receive new spiritual *bodies…*
Both the living and those who have died.

Although we cannot now know
The nature of those new bodies
They're to be glorious, by Paul we are told…

They'll be unique and incorruptible
As our GOD has chosen
For the faithful sheep within His fold. **

*** II Peter 1:13, 14 (NKJV)**
**** I Corinthians 15:35-58**

by: John A. McKee
December 13, 2005

Come out of the Darkness

Many centuries have passed
Since the creation of man
And we *still* haven't gotten it right.

We remain in the dark
Through our sinful behavior…
Found wanting in GOD's holy sight.

Just what will it take
For us to walk in the Light?
How long will GOD withhold His wrath?

He sent His Son, the Lord Jesus,
Here to save us from sin…
As '*…a Light unto my path*'. *

Mortal life quickly ends
Vanishing just as a vapor…
Yet, so many are oblivious to death.

Preferring darkness to Light…
They follow vain evil lusts
Until they gasp their very last breath.

If you repent and accept Christ
You shall surely be saved…
But unbelievers who nurture evil desire…

Who completely disregard
The warnings from Jesus
Are to be cast into the Lake of Fire. **

Jesus said watch for the signs
When He'll return as a thief
In power and glory to claim His Church Bride.

He describes events to take place
That lead up to that day
When He calls us to come to His side. ***

"The harvest is plentiful
"But the laborers are few…"
Christ said to Disciples with Him. ****

We're to witness to those
Who now walk in the darkness…
And take the *'Good News'* of Jesus to them.

*** Psalm 119:105**
**** Rev 20:11-15**
***** Matthew 24**
****** Matthew 9:37**

by: John A. McKee
December 25, 2005

Fresco - Last Judgment - 1306
Cappella Scrovegni
(Arena Chapel), Padua

Enter by the Narrow Gate

My favorite bible verse
Is that of *John 3:16*
Which states what we are to do *

To inherit life everlasting
In the Kingdom of Heaven
When our time upon this earth is through.

Many profess to be Christian,
But lust after the world…
Sinning willfully time and again.

GOD provides opportunities
To turn from evil ways
But they refuse to repent of their sin.

GOD is patient …yet jealous.
Slow to anger…yet wrathful.
He's a loving GOD quick to forgive.

He gave His only Son, Jesus,
So that believers who love Him
Shall not perish…but forever shall live.

GOD didn't send His Son here
To judge us on earth…
No, He sent Him that we might be saved.

Believers shall not be judged.
Unbelievers are judged *already*
For the evil ways they have behaved.

Jesus said, ***"I am the Way,"***
"And the Truth, and the Life…
"No one comes to the Father, but through me." **

He is the *Gate to GOD's Kingdom*.
The Way is narrow and hard…
All entering there will surely agree.

"Enter by the Narrow Gate…"
Jesus preached to the crowd,
"…Those who find it " He told them, ***"are few."***

The gate that leads to destruction
Is wide open and easy…
And many will take that avenue. ***

*** John 3:16**
**** John 14:6**
***** Matthew 7:13-14**

by: John A. McKee
January 4, 2006

Slipping the Bonds

At our appointed time,
We'll slip from these bonds
That have kept us tied here since birth…

And return home to Heaven
From whence we came
Before our temporary assignment on earth.

We have witnessed for Jesus
To those lost in darkness…
As reflectors of His Holy Light.

Now, with our *'Mission Accomplished'*
We can go to our rest
In the knowledge…*we have fought the good fight.*

Christ's last command to us
Before He ascended to Heaven
To sit at the Father's right hand…

Was to, ***"Go into all the world,***
"And preach the Gospel…" *
Spread His *'Good News'* throughout the land.

Remain steadfast to the end
And when we go home to Jesus
Beyond the farthest reaches of sky…

He'll quote from His parable…
"Well done, good and faithful servant…" **
While His Angels sing softly nearby.

Oh, what a glorious *celebration*…
As we again meet with loved ones
Who slipped their fragile bonds long before.

We'll live in *GOD's Holy City*…
Sing His praise without ceasing…
Bask in His joyous peace evermore.

*** Mark 16:15**
**** Matthew 25:14-30**

by: John A. McKee
January 13, 2006

*Martyrdom of Saint Stephen
Illustration by Gustave Dore' (1832-1883)*

* *Church historian, Schumacher researched the lives of the apostles and recounted the history of their martyrdoms.*
The details of the martyrdoms of the disciples and apostles are found in traditional early church sources. These traditions were recounted in the writings of the church fathers and the first official church history written by the historian Eusebius in A.D. 325.
Although we cannot at this time verify every detail historically, the universal belief of the early Christian writers was that each of the apostles had faced martyrdom faithfully without denying their faith in the resurrection of Jesus Christ (by Grant R. Jeffrey - an excerpt from his book "The Signature of GOD"). **http://www.direct.ca/trinity/disciples.html**

Saint Stephen – Martyred

Stephen was the first chosen
To be ordained by Apostles
As a Deacon to serve at the tables.

Full of power and grace
He performed great signs and wonders
Only GOD's Holy Spirit enables.

This was to cause a dispute
Between Stephen and others
Which his antagonists were not to win.

For Stephen possessed such great wisdom
From the Spirit within…
That he was plotted against by these men.

The scribes and the elders…
Stirred up the people
Which led to Saint Stephen's arrest.

He was brought before council
Charged with blaspheming GOD
To which accusers would falsely attest.

Narrating Jewish history
From Abraham through Solomon…
He shocked them with his summation…

"You are a stiff-necked people…"
"…The Righteous One's murderers…"
He enraged them by his accusation.

Then, the Spirit-filled Stephen
Gazed at Jesus in Heaven
As He stood at the Father's right hand.

But when he told them his vision
They stopped their ears as they rushed him…
"Stone him!" was their angry demand.

"Lord Jesus receive my spirit…"
"…Do not hold this sin against them.."
Stephen loudly prayed with his last breath.

And standing nearby observing
Was the man…*Saul of Tarsus*…
Consenting to Saint Stephen's death.

*** Acts 6:1- 8:1**

by: John A. McKee
January 17, 2006

The Martyrdom of Saint Matthew –
by Caravaggio

** Church historian, Schumacher researched the lives of the apostles and recounted the history of their martyrdoms. The details of the martyrdoms of the disciples and apostles are found in traditional early church sources. These traditions were recounted in the writings of the church fathers and the first official church history written by the historian Eusebius in A.D. 325.*

Although we cannot at this time verify every detail historically, the universal belief of the early Christian writers was that each of the apostles had faced martyrdom faithfully without denying their faith in the resurrection of Jesus Christ.(by Grant R. Jeffrey - an excerpt from his book "The Signature of GOD") http://www.direct.ca/trinity/disciples.html.

Martyrdom of Four Apostles

When the Lord Jesus Christ
Called His twelve Disciples
Their vocations were many and varied.

The tax collector Christ chose
Raised the eyebrows of many
For the stigma that hated job carried.

But that tax-man was faithful…
For he spread the Gospel
Until his death from a wound by a sword.

Saint Matthew died a brave martyr…
Back-stabbed in Ethiopia
While he was in prayer to his Lord. *

Mark joined Paul and Barnabas,
On their mission to Cyprus…
He was also Saint Peter's good friend.

Dragged in Alexandria, Egypt
Through the streets behind horses
Is the way Saint Mark's life was to end. *

The physician, Luke, was beloved
Among the martyred Apostles…
He accompanied Saint Paul to Rome.

Saint Luke led many to Christ
Through his tremendous preaching
And they hung him for that far from home. *

John faced martyrdom in Rome
When he was boiled in oil…
But through a miracle Saint John was spared.

He wrote, *'the Revelation to John'*
While confined on Patmos
Jesus showed John the vision he shared. *

by: John A. McKee
January 20, 2006

Saint Peter is often depicted in art holding the keys to the kingdom of heaven.

** Church historian, Schumacher researched the lives of the apostles and recounted the history of their martyrdoms.*

The details of the martyrdoms of the disciples and apostles are found in traditional early church sources. These traditions were recounted in the writings of the church fathers and the first official church history written by the historian Eusebius in A.D. 325.Although we cannot at this time verify every detail historically, the universal belief of the early Christian writers was that each of the apostles had faced martyrdom faithfully without denying their faith in the resurrection of Jesus Christ.

(by Grant R. Jeffrey - an excerpt from his book "The Signature of GOD") http://www.direct.ca/trinity/disciples.html.

Martyrdom of Peter and Andrew

"Follow me," said Christ Jesus
To Simon and Andrew,
"And I'll make you fishers of men."

They both dropped their nets
To immediately follow…
And they were never the same men again.

Impetuous Peter *loved* Jesus,
As did all the Disciples,
And the Lord Jesus loved them in turn.

He was their Master…their Mentor…
Their Lord and their Teacher…
Teaching them things He wants *us* to learn.

The brothers *did* learn their lessons…
For they picked up His banner
After Lord Jesus had been crucified.

Peter went into the world
To spread the Gospel to Gentiles
And while in Rome, heroic Saint Peter died.

Nero ordered him crucified
Upon an x-shaped cross…
Upside down as Saint Peter had requested.

He told his Roman tormentors,
He felt unworthy to die
As did Jesus after He was arrested. *

Andrew was crucified in Greece,
On an x-shaped cross also…
Calling it *'the happy hour he most desired.'*

Saint Andrew preached the Good News
For two days to tormentors…
Until he gave up the ghost…and expired. *

by: John A. McKee
January 23, 2006

Saint James the Greater

** Church historian, Schumacher researched the lives of the apostles and recounted the history of their martyrdoms. The details of the martyrdoms of the disciples and apostles are found in traditional early church sources. These traditions were recounted in the writings of the church fathers and the first official church history written by the historian Eusebius in A.D. 325. Although we cannot at this time verify every detail historically, the universal belief of the early Christian writers was that each of the apostles had faced martyrdom faithfully without denying their faith in the resurrection of Jesus Christ.(by Grant R. Jeffrey - an excerpt from his book "The Signature of GOD") http://www.direct.ca/trinity/disciples.html.*

Martyrs for Christ

Christ's half brother, James…
Known as, *'James the Just'*…
Became Bishop of Jerusalem.

He was martyred for refusing
To deny the Lord Jesus…
And would die before renouncing Him.

Thrown from a high pinnacle
Over one hundred feet down…
Though badly injured, he was still alive.

Saint James' vicious enemies
Then clubbed him severely
And this cruelty…he was not to survive.

James *the Greater* was a fisherman
With his young brother, John…
The sons of Salome and Zebedee.

A loyal Disciple for Jesus,
And very strong Church leader
Was this Saint James from Galilee.

When arrested for his faith,
His Roman officer guard
Was amazed by him during the trial.

Defending his faith took great courage
But he loved the Lord Jesus
And this loyalty he would never defile.

The Spirit convicted the officer
When Saint James was condemned
Within his heart, the Holy Spirit imbedded.

As he declared *his* new faith,
He knelt down next to James,
And the judge ordered *both* men beheaded. *

by: John A. McKee
January 25, 2006

93

"St. Jude Thaddeus," by: Georges de La Tour c .1615- 1620. Oil on canvas. Musée Toulouse-Lautrec: Albi, France.

** Church historian, Schumacher researched the lives of the apostles and recounted the history of their martyrdoms.*

The details of the martyrdoms of the disciples and apostles are found in traditional early church sources. These traditions were recounted in the writings of the church fathers and the first official church history written by the historian Eusebius in A.D. 325. Although we cannot at this time verify every detail historically, the universal belief of the early Christian writers was that each of the apostles had faced martyrdom faithfully without denying their faith in the resurrection of Jesus Christ.

(by Grant R. Jeffrey - an excerpt from his book "The Signature of GOD") http://www.direct.ca/trinity/disciples.html.

Four Martyred Apostles

Before Philip led him to Christ,
Bartholomew (called Nathanael),
Was known for his Nazareth quip…

Nathanael was martyred in Armenia
For converting their King.
He was flayed to death there with a whip. *

The Disciple, Thomas (the Doubter),
Founded a Church in Babylon…
Then went to Persia and India to preach.

He built a great many Churches
Throughout his ministry
Making converts of all he could reach.

Saint Thomas traveled worldwide
Bringing sinners to Christ…
Daily preaching GOD's Word without fear.

But, on his last trip to India
To build a new church…
He died when pierced through by a spear. *

Jude, a Disciple of Jesus,
Preached in several countries
Fervently bringing *'Good News'* to the lost.

Although martyred in Persia
For his faith in Christ Jesus…
Jude's reward far exceeded his cost. *

The traitor, Judas Iscariot
Was replaced by Matthias
Whose evangelistic skills became honed…

For more than thirty years he preached
From Judea to Ethiopia
Until at Colchis…Saint Matthias was stoned. *

*** John 1:45-46**

by: John A. McKee
January 30, 2006

To order additional copies of this book...

POEMS OF PRAISE VOLUME II
Please have your credit card ready and call
1 800-917-BOOK (2665)

Or order by e-mail at:
orders@selahbooks.com

You may also place book orders online at
www.selahbooks.com

Printed in the United States
200071BV00004B/211-258/A